THE REIGN, THE FALL AND THE REBIRTH OF A NATION

OREOLUWA A. OLALEYE

DEDICATION

To the once upon a time "Giant of Africa"

Author's Note

The Reign, the Fall and the Rebirth of a Nation is the story of Nigeria. Nigeria is introduced to the reader/audience as the giant of Africa, a beauty to behold. Her geopolitical zones, people, cultures, resources, food, and most of her strengths are mentioned in details. Unfortunately, her strengths are not the only thing there is to her.

A foreign nation, represented by two men in white, came to one of her chiefs (a village chief), who sold Nigeria to them in exchange for a mirror. This saddens Nigeria greatly as most of her treasures were looted. This incidence was the first of many woes that befell Nigeria as a nation. Her identity was stolen from her, and worse maladies arose – selfishness, corruption, lack of love, perverseness, hatred, wickedness and greediness.

In the Southern, Eastern, Northern and Western regions of Nigeria, these gross sins led to disunity, insecurity, killings, rape, violence, insurrection, pollution of the land, poverty, unemployment, alarming increase in crime rate, injustice, grief, and more. This eventually causes Nigeria to break down and she falls, heartbroken and bloodstained from the sins that are flourishing in her as a Nation. The cry, "Nigeria is fallen", rings through the crowd as the citizens gather around the once upon a time "giant of Africa".

A voice is then heard, admonishing the people, telling them to let go of what caused the current misfortune – nepotism, tribalism, injustice, lack of love, apathy and so on. They are advised to "come as one" and lift Nigeria high, to "be her pillar and her support" till she returns to her state of former glory and even   more.

Enters a lady dressed in a long, flowy green, white, green on stage – representing Nigeria. She is adorned in beautiful jewelries – a crown of beads, beads on the neck, wrists, waist and ankles. She carries a basket filled with fruits to show the fruitfulness of the nation, parading as praises are being showered on her by the Orator.

ORATOR: Nigeria,

Dear Nigeria,

The giant of Africa,

Regal, majestic, beautiful.

Stunning beyond all words,

Who can compare to her allure?

Endowed with treasures no woman's jewelry box can

hold,

Who can hold a candle to her?

Strong, she was,

A queen in her own right.

Colorful with wondrous array of diverse cultures,

Her people were her strength.

Intelligent, wise, geniuses in every way,

Brilliant, strong and gorgeous in a way that no poet could

ever find enough ways to describe with words.

Their beauty is both superficial and bone deep.

Their songs incited feelings of home,

Enveloping one in a cocoon of warmth.

Their proverbs were filled with ancient wisdom,

That opened the eyes and humbled the heart.

They were one with nature,

Living prosperous and healthy lives.

These were the ways of the people.

Four (4) individuals, two (2) males and two (2) females, dressed in 4

different cultural attires representing the West (Yoruba), East (Igbo),

North (Hausa-Fulani), and South (Niger Deltas). They parade the stage, dancing round Nigeria to a cultural beat heard in the background, before arraying themselves in front of her. Each person takes turns to address the audience, boasting about what their regions/tribes are best known for.

NORTH:(greets the audience in general Hausa)

Barka da rana jama'a

I stand for the North.

Out of the six geopolitical zones in Nigeria,

Three are northern zones,

Namely the North-central, North-east and the North-west.

There are six (6) states in each zone.

With the inclusion of Abuja which is the Federal Capital Territory (FCT),

It makes it a total of 19 Northern states.

The States in the North Central include Benue, Kogi, Kwara, Nasarawa, Niger and Plateau States.

The FCT is also found in this zone.

The states in the North-east zones are Adamawa, Bauchi. Borno, Gombe, Taraba and Yobe states.

The states in the North West are Jigawa, Kaduna, Kano, Katsina, Kebbi, Sokoto and Zamfara states.

In the, the majority is Hausa-Fulani,

Although there are many other tribes aside from Hausa-Fulani.

A few of them are Achipa, Affade, Amo. Anaguta, Ataka, Babur, Bachama, Bada, Bali, Bambora, Bandawa, Banka, Banso. Bara, Barke, Baruba, Bashiri, Bassa, Baushi, Baya, Belewa, Billle, Birom, Bobua, Bussawa, Bolewa, Boma, Bomboro, Buduwa, Buji, Bunu, Burak, Bwatiye, Chamba, Chibok, Chokobo, Chukkol, Daba, Dadiya, Dakarkari, Dangsa, Daza, Dumuk, Egede (igedde), Fyem, Ga'anda, Galambi, Gamergu-Mulgwa, Gbedde, Gera, Geruma, Gira, Goernai, Gurmana, Gwa, Gwandara, Higi, Idoma, Igala, Jere, Jombo, Jukun, Kaba, Kafanchan, Kamaku,

Kambari, Kanuri, Karekare, Kurama, Kwanka, Longuda, Mundang, Ngamo, Ninzam, Nupe, Ogori, Oworo, Palli, Pulbe, Qanawuri, Rindire, Segidi, Shuwa, Tarok, Terawa, Tiv, Uncinda, Verre, Waja, Yagba, Zulawa and so on.

I am the food basket of the Nation.

Though the climate borders of the extremes (both cold and heat),

The land is fertile and bears rich and nutritious grains, tubers, fruits and vegetables such as yam, cassava, beans, rice, groundnut, tomatoes, bell peppers, carrots, onions, orange, mango, Pineapple and much more.

The North is rich in mineral resources like Copper, Baryte, Columbite, Dolomite, Lead, Zinc, Gold, Tin, Cocoa, Cotton, Talc, Marble, Limestone, Iron-ore, Gypsium, Cassiterite, Uranium, Bentonite, Gemstones to mention but a few.

Our native meals include (but are not limited to) Tuwo Shinkafa, Masa, Killishi, Nakiya, Yar Tsala, Kunun Gyda, and Danbu.

Every single one of our meals are rich in nutrients that are beneficial for human health.

With the above mentioned, you will be right to say that we are not just farmers and illiterates,

We are more,

We are AREWA.[1]

EAST: (greets the audience in general Igbo)

Cha cha cha Igbo kwenu! (twice) Kwezuo Nu![2]

I am the East., representing the Igbos.

Of the six (6) geopolitical zones in Nigeria,

The South-East belongs to the Igbos,

Consisting of Abia, Anambra, Ebonyi, Enugu and Imo states.

Although collectively known as Igbos, there are many subgroups such as Anioma, Aro, Ekpeye, Ezza, Ibeku,

---

[1] Hausa language meaning "Northerners"

[2] This way of greeting is strictly for men in the igbo land. An igbo woman greets as thus, "Ndi beanyi ekene munu!" or "Ndewo nu o"

Ikwerre, Isu, Mbaise, Ngwa, Ogba, Ohafia, Omuma, Oyigbo, and so on.

Our females are beautiful and our men handsome.

We are hardworking and strong, known for our prowess in the business sector

The Igbos are kings when it comes to the business area of our nation, Nigeria, due to our entrepreneur skills. Some say we are cunning, but we pride ourselves in our Wisdom.

Our mineral resources include (but are not limited to) Coal, salt, Lead, Zinc, Gypsium, Lignite, Marcasite, Gold, Limestone, Glass-sand, and phosphate.

We are well known for our variety of delicious soups, Soups like Egusi, Ogbono, Ofe Onugbu (Bitter-leaf soup), Okra soup, Oha soup, Ofaku and so on.

Other foods native to Igbo land include Abacha, Echicha, Isi Ewu, Nkwobi, Nsala, Okpa, Fio Fio, Ukwa and many more.

Igbo Kwenu!

We are the pillar of the Nation.

WEST: (greets the audience in general Yoruba)

Mo ki yin ooo gbogboo eyin ilumoye, (I greet you all)

Asi ku ojo oni (congratulations on seeing the present day).

I represent the West, the Yoruba(s).

Of the six (6) geopolitical zones in Nigeria, the South-West belongs to the Yoruba Kingdom,

Having six (6) states which are Ekiti, Lagos, Ogun, Ondo, Osun, and Oyo states.

Few know of the subtribes in the Yoruba Kingdom and they are the Ana people, Anago tribe, Awori tribe, Ebirra (or Igbira) people, Egba kingdom, Egbado (also known as Yewa people), Egun, Ekiti people, Ibarapa people, Idaasha people, Igbomina people,

Ijebu Kingdom, Ijesha, Ijumu tribe, Ikale tribe, Ilaje tribe, Isa people, Isaosa people, Isha people, Ketu, Ohori people, Okun people, Onko people, Oworo people, Owu people, Sabe people, Yagba people, and so on.

I am glad to tell you all that God has blessed us a lot.

In mineral resources, there is Gold, Crude Oil, Bitumen, Granite, Kaolin, Tatium, Syenite, Feldspar, Clay, Glass-Sand, Limestone, Phosphate, Coal, Gypsum, Gemstone, Columbite, Talc, Tantalite, Tourmaline, Aqua Marine, Casserite, Dolomite, Marble, And So On.

In Agriculture, the land is blessed with food, fruits, vegetables and raw materials such as Timber, Rubber, Plantain, Cassava, Yam, Cocoyam, Rice, Mangoes, Oranges, Tropical Almond, Groundnut, Palm kernels, Coconuts, Cocoa, and so on.

We have a lot of native food that is nourishing,

Obe Gbegiri and Ewedu (beans soup and jute leaves),

Efo Riro (vegetable soup), obe Egusi pelu Isapa (Egusi

soup with dried okra), Ila Alasepo (Okra soup), Iyan

(pounded yam), Eba (Garri), Amala (yam/cassava

flour), and so on pupuru.

We are known for our respectful culture, for our love

for education, for humility and morality.

Eyin omo Oduduwa!

We are the peace of the Nation.

SOUTH: (greets the audience in a southern language)

I proudly represent the southern part of Nigeria, also

known as The Niger Delta.

The South-south geopolitical zone, with its six (6)

states – Akwa Ibom, Bayelsa, Cross River, Delta, Edo

and Rivers states, belong to the people of the south.

In the south, the tribes present are more than one

can imagine.

For example, there are the Abayon, Abua, Agbo, Akajuk, Anang, Andoni, Anyima, Bachere, Bahumono, Bekwara, Bette, Bille, Boki, Ebana, Ebu, Edo, Efik, Egbema, Egede, Egbira, Ekajuk, Eket, Ekoi, Ekpeye, Engenni, Esit Ekid, Etche, Etsako, Etung, Etuno, Gokana, Ibani, Ibeno, Ibibios, Igede, Ijaw (Izon), Ika, Ikom, Ikwerre, Iman, Ishan, Isoko, Itsekiri, Itu Mbio uso, Kalabari, Kwale, Kugbo, Mbembe, Nkim, Ododop, Ogoni, Ogba, Okirika, Okobo, Okpamheri, Olukumi, Oron, Ososo, Owan, Qua, Udekeama, Uhrobo, Ukelle, Uneme, Uyanga, Weppa-wanno, Yache, Yakurr and many more.

The south is known as the economic mainstream of Nigeria,

We are rich in minerals, water and forest resources such as Timber, Clay, Lead, Zinc. Limestone, Oil/Gas, Salt, Uranium, Marble, Glass-Sand, Gypsum, Iron-Ore,

Kaolin, Lignite, Bitumen, Dolomite, Gold, Barite, Manganese and so on.

We are known for our fishery as we are surrounded by water bodies.

We have divers' kinds of delicious and mouthwatering indigenous meals such as Banga, Edikang Ikong, Afang, Ofe Akwu, Ogbono Soup, Black Soup, White Soup, Fisherman's Soup, Owo Soup, Kekefia, Onunu, Ukodo, Ikwerre Native Soup, to mention but a few.

Let me stop there to prevent over salivation.

Our dressing nko, we dress like the kings and queens that we are.

Abegi, South south, we are too much.

All four parade out of the stage, leaving only Nigeria.

ORATOR: how about the land,

The fertile soil?

The beauty of the land in various parts,

Whether south or east,

North or south,

It brought tears to the eyes of all who cared to see,

It wrung sighs of awe and bliss out of the lips of the

admirers,

The land brought forth more than one could

imagine,

Rich we were in minerals,

Gold, iron ore, tin, limestone, crude oil, lead, zinc,

Talc, bitumen, granite, silver, coal

The list goes on and on.

How about food?

Diverse food and fruits filled our markets and

tables,

Exotic and tropical,

Delicious, both to the eyes and tongue.

(Deep sad sigh)

But Alas!

Like is seen in great world civilizations brought to

ruin,

Selfishness,

With all its rottenness,

Sprung up in the hearts of the people,

Both foreign and local.

Hmmmm,

Selfishness became common,

Seen everywhere,

In every corner,

In every nook and cranny.

Our land was plundered,

We were stolen from, subjugated,

And our identity was taken from us.

A village chief enters the stage and introduces himself as one of the major chiefs in a Tribe in Nigeria. Two men dressed in white, enter the stage after the Chief. An exchange is seen occurring between the Chief and the other two men; the chief is given a mirror, who in turn gives them the key that unlocks the basket in the hands of Nigeria. The Chief leaves the stage and the men in white go to Nigeria, unlock the basket and take away all that is in it. Nigeria wears a sad expression as this happens.

ORATOR: (in a grave voice)

> This was the beginning of our woes.
>
> Selfishness, together with corruption,
>
> Lack of love, perverseness,
>
> Hatred and greediness,
>
> With all its dirty chubby hands created a storm,
>
> A storm so large, it threatens to consume all,
>
> If actions are not taken to disperse it hastily.

Slowly but surely,

Disunity arose,

Insecurity now threatens all.

In the south, east, north and west,

Evil prevails.

Our mothers are not safe,

Our daughters and sister hide out of fear.

Our fathers, brothers and husbands walk in haste,

Looking over their shoulders every minute.

Our youths,

Oh, our dear youths,

They are left to suffer,

Reaping the evil fruits of the seeds sown by the

mistakes of our fathers.

For them, it has become kill or be killed,

Their blood flows freely down our streets and our

elders turn a blind eye to this evil.

This evil daily kill our beloved nation,

Weakening her and bringing her to her knees.

Our gallant nation looks to the South,

And what does she see?

Nigeria turns slowly towards a group of three southerners (two females and a male), who can be heard mumbling, with sad expressions and angry voices. The females are both with empty calabashes, and the male is with a fishing-net.

FEMALE 1: (almost in tears, lamenting)

Oh Lord!

There is no good water anywhere!

(Raises calabash to show its empty)

The water is stained!

It's making me and my children sick!

Look at my body (points to exposed hands covered

with sores and blisters),

I got this from trying to manage the water last week.

FEMALE 2: (angrily)

My sister, hmmm,

I can't cook with the water too o.

The last time I tried it, my family suffered dearly for

it.

Our waters are poisoned.

To top it off, the major occupation,

Our pride, which is Fishery, has been reduced to

almost nothing as the fishes die off due to the

pollution of our water bodies.

My husband heads out each day and returns empty

handed!

How are we going to survive?

I find it difficult to cater for the needs of my children

Even school fees, I can't pay.

My small child asked me a question recently, and I

was heartbroken

He asked me, 'mummy, are we going to die?'

I couldn't answer him (in shame)

MALE: Our people say that a man that cannot feed His

family is worse than an infidel

They say that men do not cry (eyes heavy with tears)

Why won't I cry when I am worse than an infidel?

I've been at sea,

All day, all night

Here is the result of all my toils

(Showing empty fishnet)

The oil spillage is killing our fishes,

Destroying our economy and leaving us hungry!

All because of our pipelines that are being

vandalized!

chai!

Exploited and suffering as a result,

Our people are now easily irritated.

As a result, we see fights here and there.

hmmm

ALL THREE: pray for divine justice and also cursing, they freeze on stage. Nigeria, listening to them from afar looking really sad.

ORATOR: (sadly)

hmmmm,

Poverty, hunger, unemployment strives

Civil workers are not paid their salaries,

Graduates litter the streets idle.

Like they say, "an idle hand is the devil's workshop".

It came as no surprise when crime rate, including

rape, cybercrimes, murder and the likes,

increased.

Youths take to the streets,

Robbing and stealing.

Unfortunately, their victims are usually people trying

to make ends meet like themselves.

She looks to the North

(Nigeria turns to the North)

Hoping to see a scene that would ease the pain in her

heart,

But again, what unfolds before her?

A family of three, a male and two females come on stage. They are seen heading to the farm with their baskets and cutlasses. They engage in casual conversations. On getting to the farm, they get to work. Two males, dressed in kaftans, turbans and masked with bandannas jump out of the bush, killing the father, raping the mother and kidnapping the daughter. The raped mother later comes out of hiding and sobs beside her dead husband. She freezes mid-sob on stage.

(Nigeria gasps in horror, clutching her chest as she is in pain)

ORATOR: this is a horror that shakes our Nation to her core and makes her bleed,

It deepens her wounds,

And drive the proverbial knife through her heart.

Herdsmen attack,

Terrorists annihilate,

Demolishing and causing ruin everywhere they go.

Fathers and sons are killed on their farmlands,

Mothers and daughters are kidnapped,

Children are orphaned and displaced from their homes.

Villages, homes to hundreds and thousands of our people, are raided, plundered and burnt.

Bombs go free,

Taking lives and destroying properties.

Lives are lost,

Causing grief upon grief,

One that nothing could ever soothe,

An ache, an empty space in our hearts,

That would remain as long as we live.

(Nigeria sobs)

And yet... no one hears the sobs of our nation.

Bleeding, weakened,

Our nation moves and slowly looks to the west.

(Nigeria turns slowly to the west)

It was the twentieth of October, two thousand and

twenty,

A day known as Black Tuesday.

A group of protesters came on stage, carrying placards and

chanting "End SARS, End corruption, End bad governance, put an

end to insecurity and so on". On getting to a certain part of the stage, they address each other, after which they start singing.

SONG: every junction police dey

Eh eh police dey (2x)

Oga where your paper

Oga where your twenty-naira ooo

Every junction police dey

Eh eh police dey

Solidarity forever (3x)

We shall always fight for our rights!

Two soldiers come on stage and try to get them to stop. It ends in a sporadic shooting, with screams and shoutings. The scene freezes. Nigeria staggers, and crumbles, her back bent, her body shaking as she sobs.

ORATOR: (sadly)

It was horrendous

It was indeed the darkest yet experienced in the once

upon a time giant of Africa.

It was a night of terror and horror beyond

description.

Screams of terror, cries of agony filled the air,

Waterfalls of tears freely flowed.

Shaky voices, salty with tears and yet brave, sang the

nation's anthem,

While the protector turned villain fired on,

Killing her people in cold blood.

This was unadulterated cruelty.

An unfortunately common case,

One where a nation kills the very people it swore to

protect,

Blood flowing freely down the streets,

The green-white-green stained with the blood of her

people.

On shaky feet, she tried to stand

Heartbroken, weakened and unable to bear the

scenes anymore,

She turns to the east.

Nigeria turns to the east where a man is seen addressing a small

group. While speaking, he is interrupted by an officer who arrests

him. The crowd, in turn, gets angry and turns violent. The scene

freezes as they (the officer and the arrested individual) step away

from the people.

ORATOR: In the east, law enforcement agencies are attacked,

By men popularly known as ungun known men

Oh, sorry pardon me,

I meant unknown gunmen.

These people, men blood flowing through their

veins,

Men with families,

Go about destroying properties,

Inciting fear in the heart of the people.

The easterners, who desire to break free from a

nation that will not listen to their voices,

Are being forced through oppression, force and

something akin to tyranny,

To pretend that they are still one with a nation they

have lost interest in.

This is a terrible mistake,

Because at the end of the day,

Things will only get worse.

Everywhere goes quiet as a banshee-like scream is heard, as it

pierces through the air. Nigeria is seen falling down. The scenes that

were paused on stage unfreeze and everyone looks around with a

confused expression. They see Nigeria lying on the floor. In shock,

they step forward one after the other.

A YORUBA MAN: ahhhhhhh!

samba fo![3]

Eerin Wo![4] (the elephant is fallen)

Nigeria ti subu! (Nigeria has fallen)

A HAUSA MAN: kai!

Nigeria ta fa gi! (Nigeria has fallen)

AN IGBO LADY: ewwwooooo!

Nigeria adago! (Nigeria has fallen)

AN AKWA-IBOM LADY: chaiii!

Nigeria adwo ooo! (Nigeria has fallen)

ORATOR: (soberly)

Hmmm indeed

---

[3] A Yoruba idiomatic expression meaning that a great misfortune has happened.
[4] A Yoruba idiomatic expression meaning that a great personality or important person has been to lost, usually through death.

Nigeria is fallen.

Listen oh my people,

(Everyone pauses as they listen)

Though Nigeria is fallen,

It is never too late to work together and make her

rise once again.

Wake up out of your reverie,

Out of your pity party,

Out of your state of numbness and apathy!

Wake up and smell the smoke,

The roof is almost on the floor !

As said by a patriotic Nigerian, Aisha Yesufu,

"It is no longer a matter of if, it is a matter of when.

Yesterday's victims were once survivors, today's

victims were yesterday's survivors and tomorrow's

victims will be today's survivors".

Come as one, You people

And lift your nation high,

Be her pillar and her support,

Till she rises again,

As the queen that she is,

The Giant of Africa.

Crowd move to help Nigeria stand. Once in an upright state, she is redecorated and lifted, sitting on the shoulders of the people as they cheer on. The people then turn to face the audience as they sing the National anthem. Everyone takes a bow.

EXEUNT

ABOUT THE AUTHOR

Oreoluwa A. Olaleye is a First-class Graduate in Human Anatomy from Adeleke University, Ede, Osun State. She is the first of 5 children. She is a Nigerian, a proud African, a Christian, a lover of nature, a poet, a voracious reader and a writer.

ABOUT THE BOOK

The book is figuratively about Nigeria; who she is, of how she came to be, her predicament, the disastrous end that could be and how to prevent it or heal her.